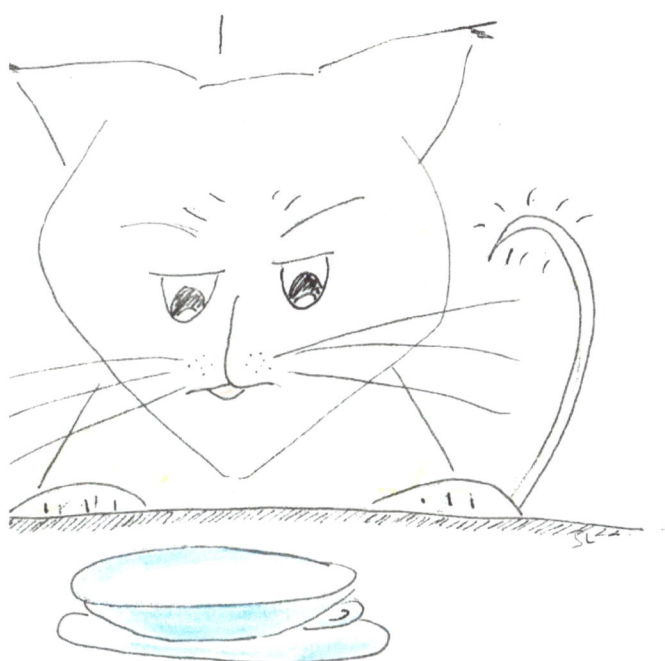

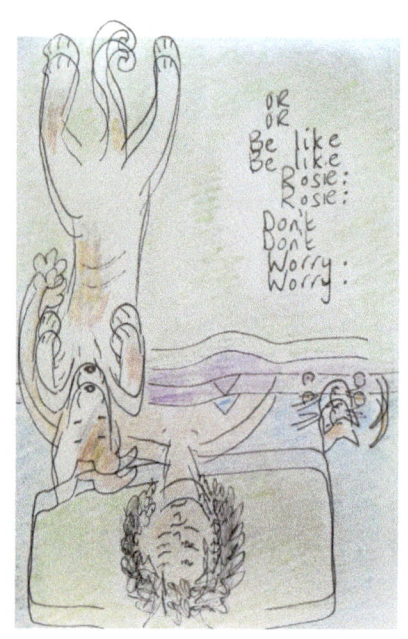

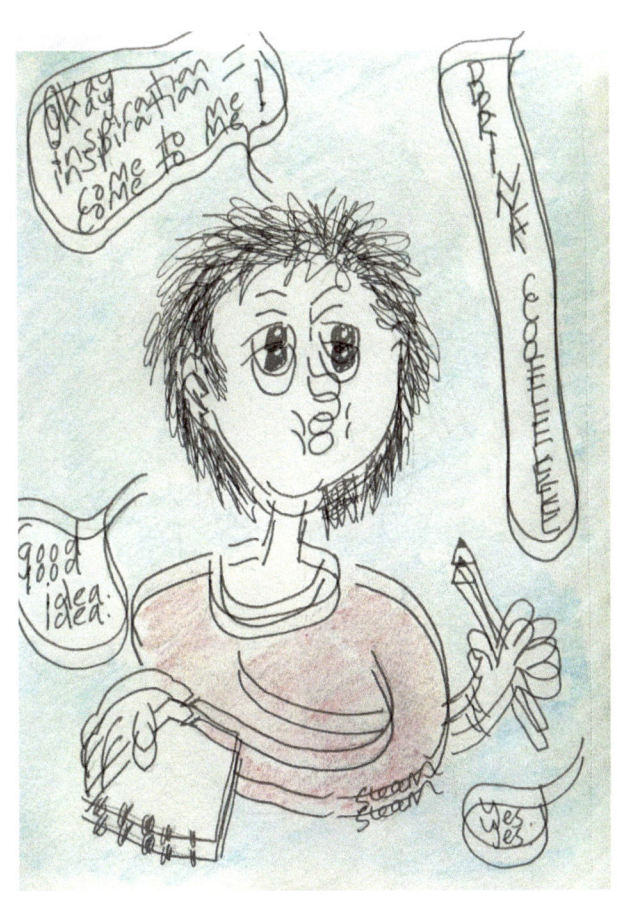

I find it odd how much my dog begs.

mmm... bagels

What was that? Salmon not Gouda today? Okay.

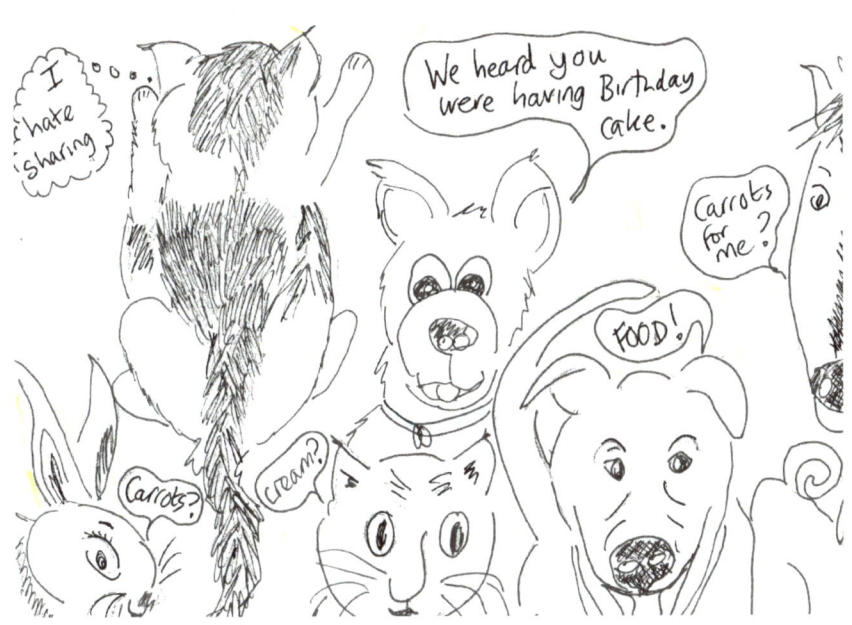

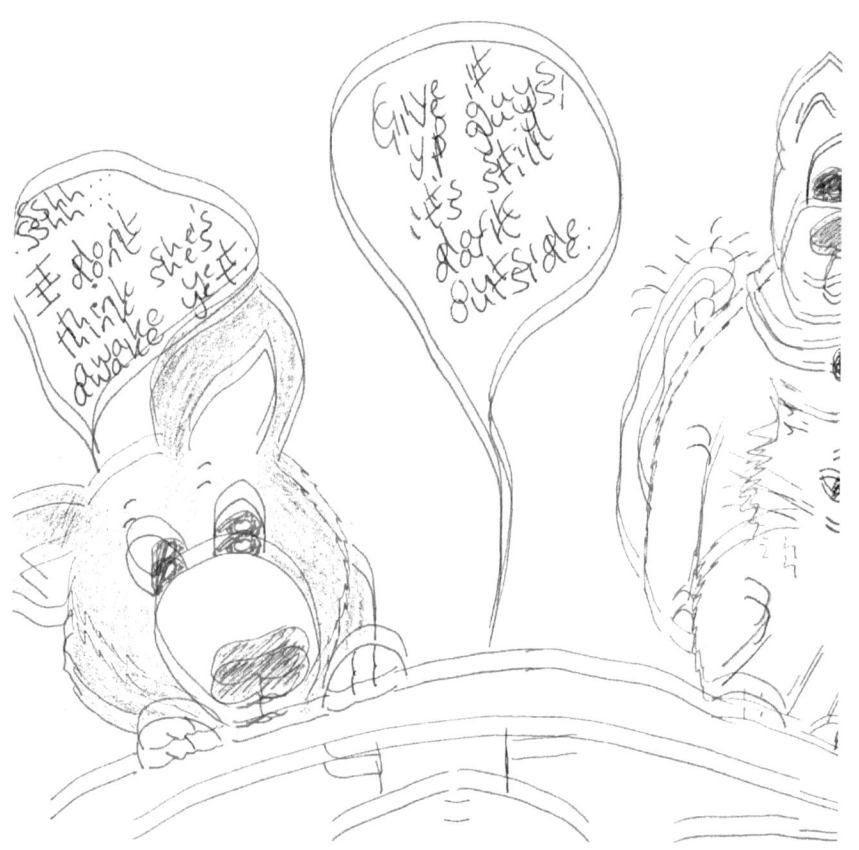

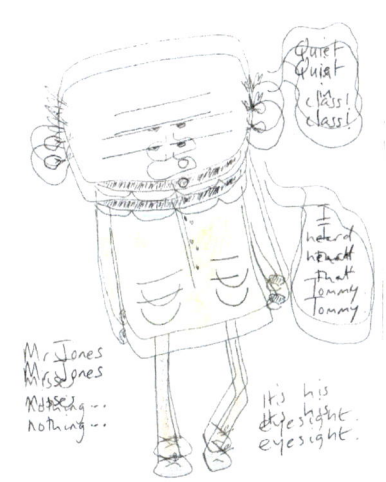

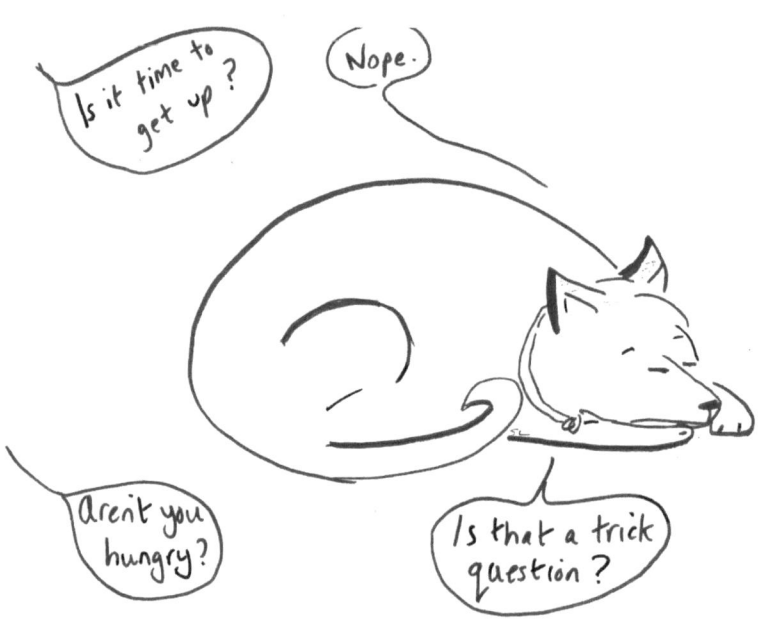

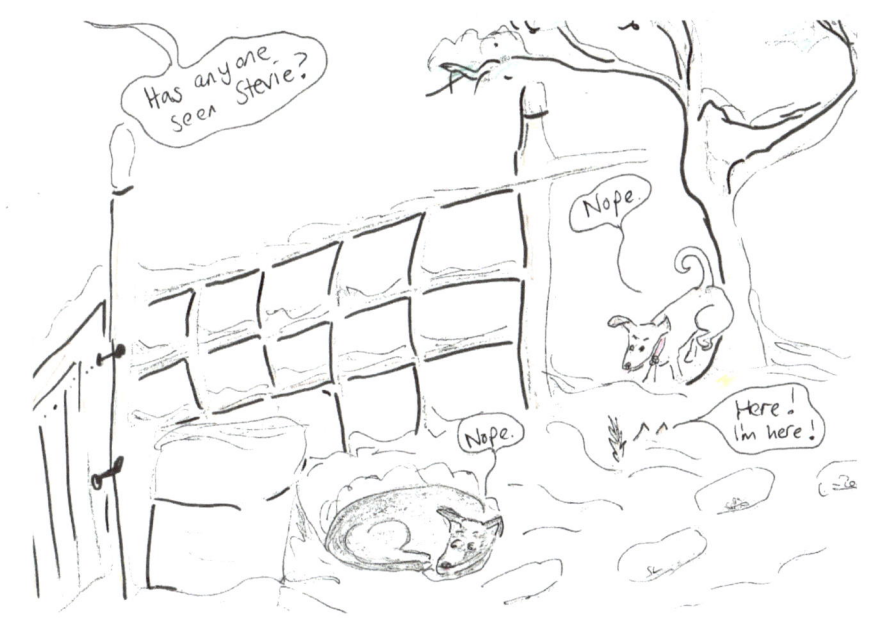

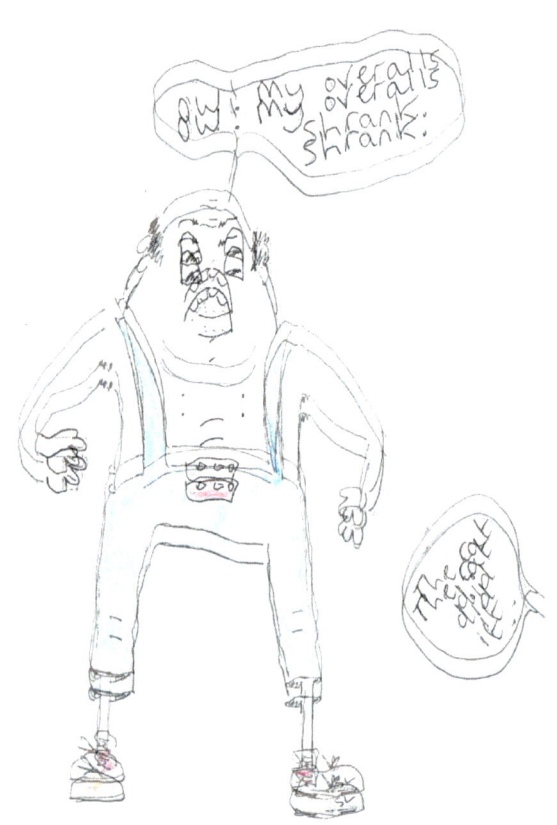

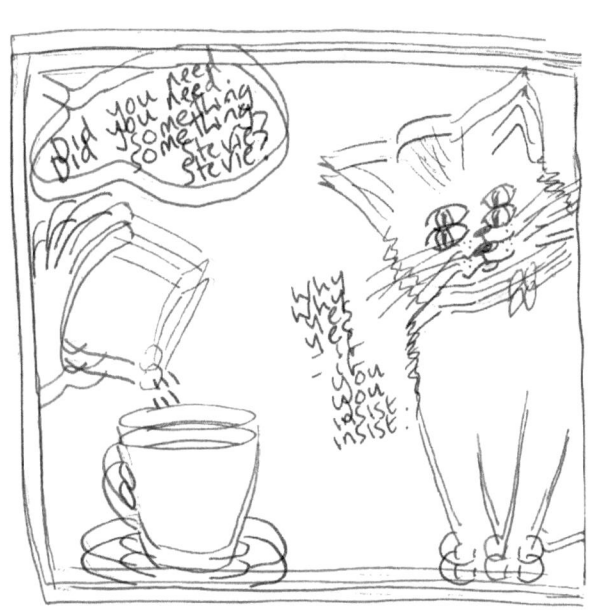

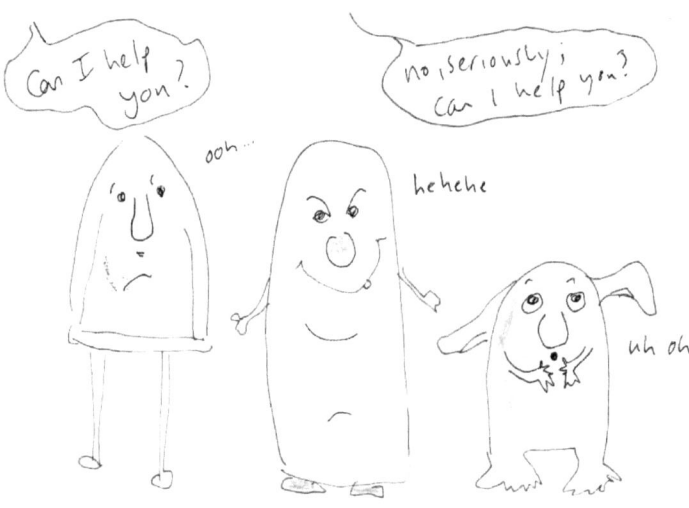

The Blob family is overwhelmed by all the choices. It's not like at home.

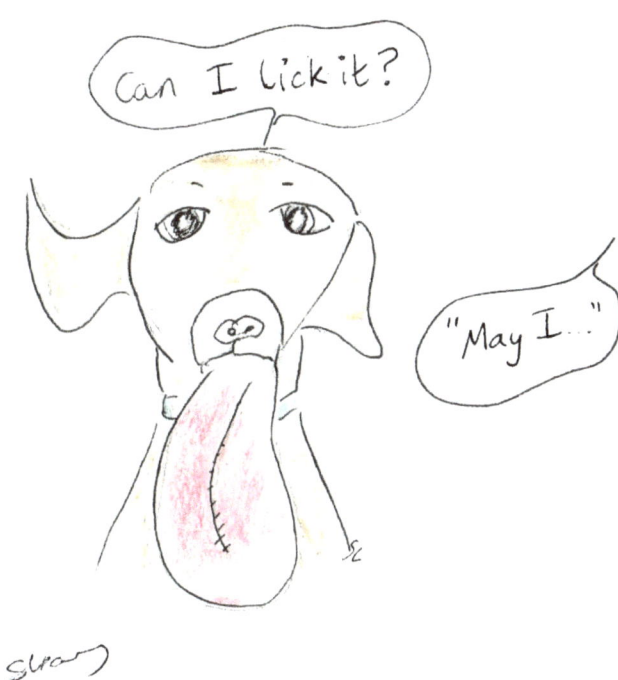

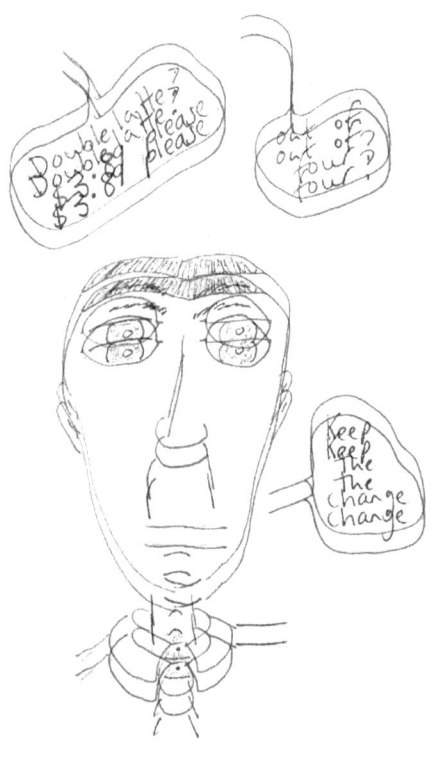

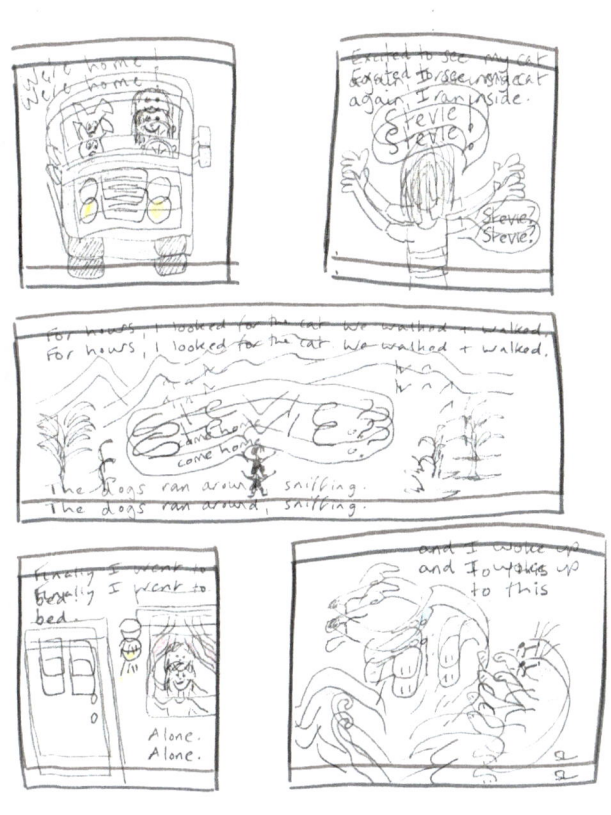

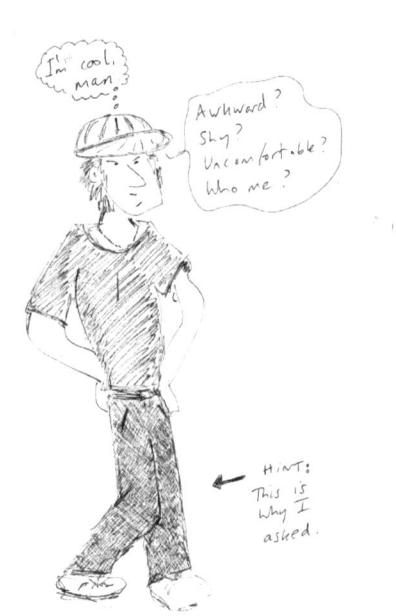

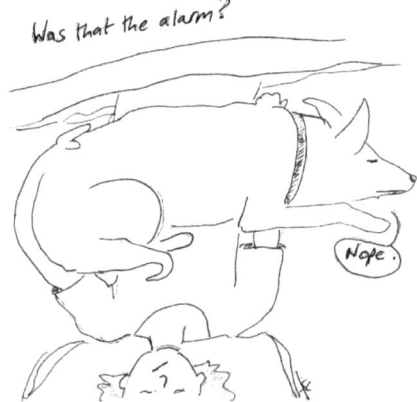

A dog. An apple.
A nap.
This is a Sunday poem.

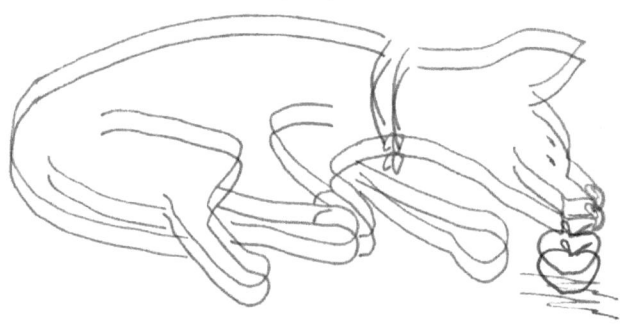

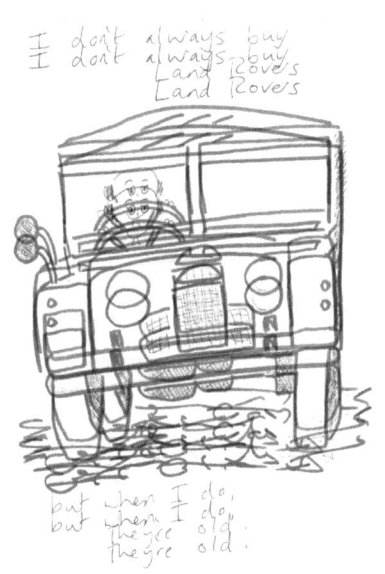

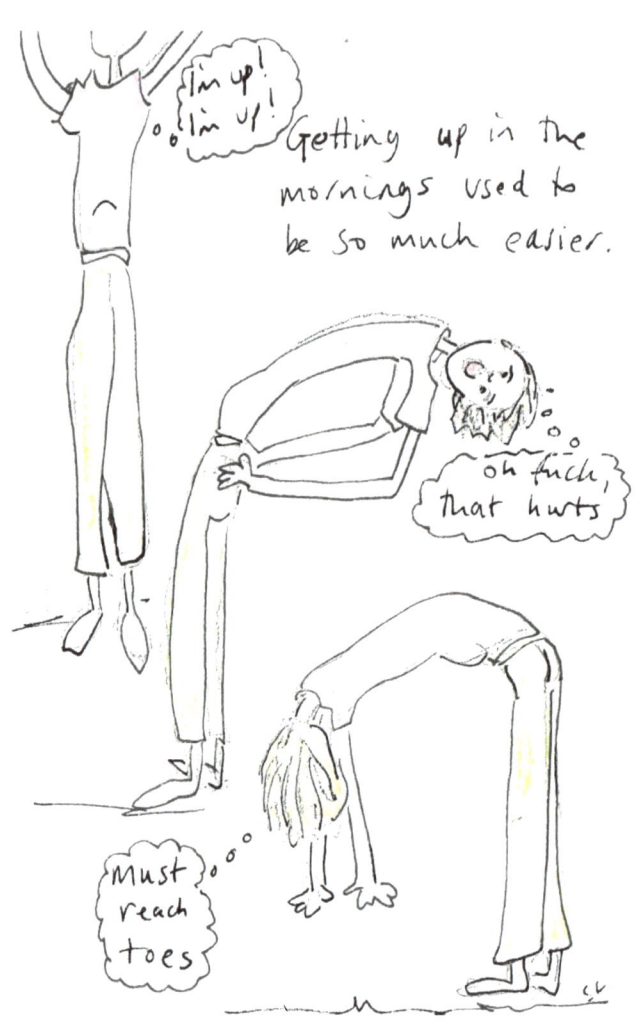

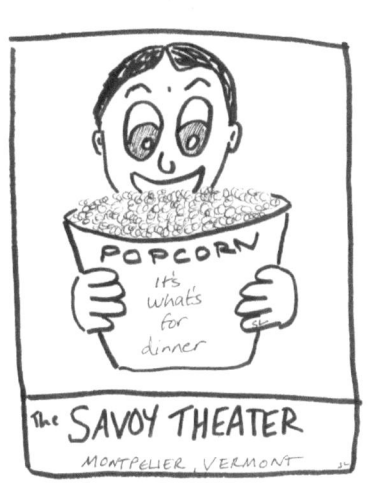

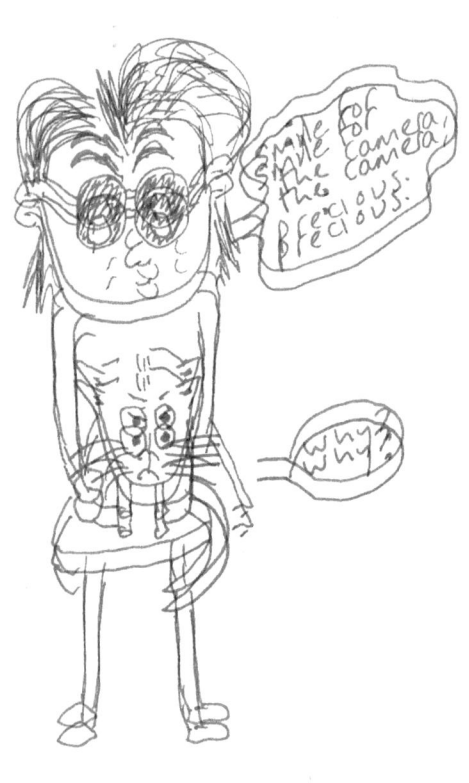

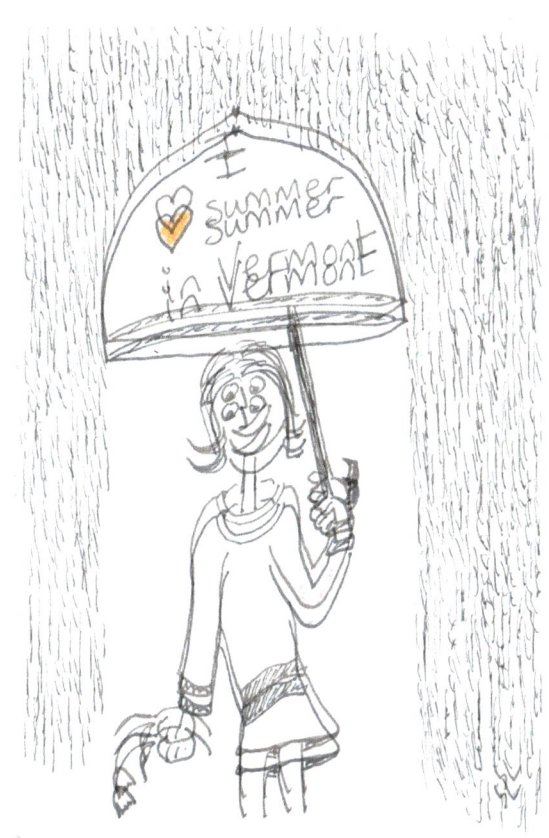

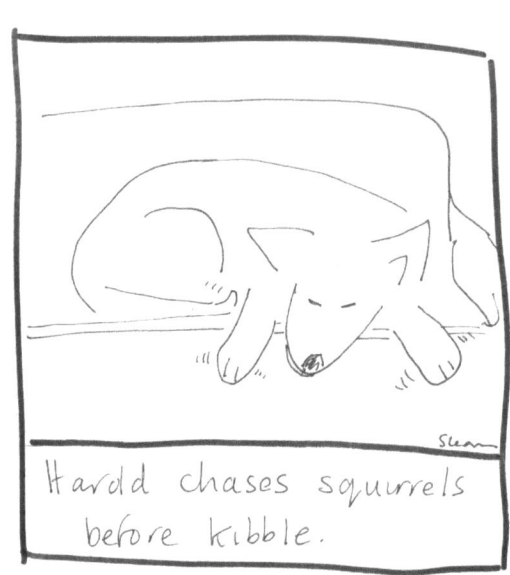

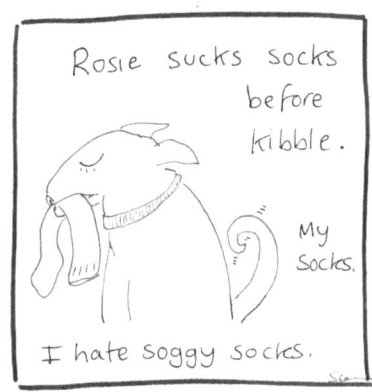

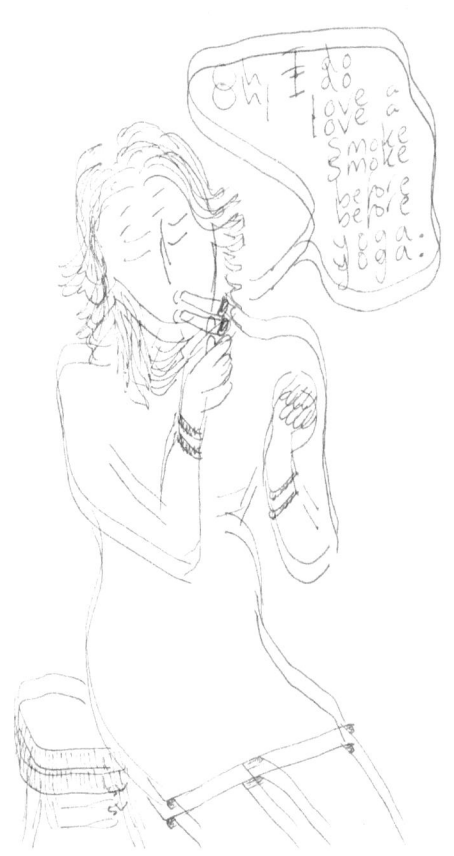

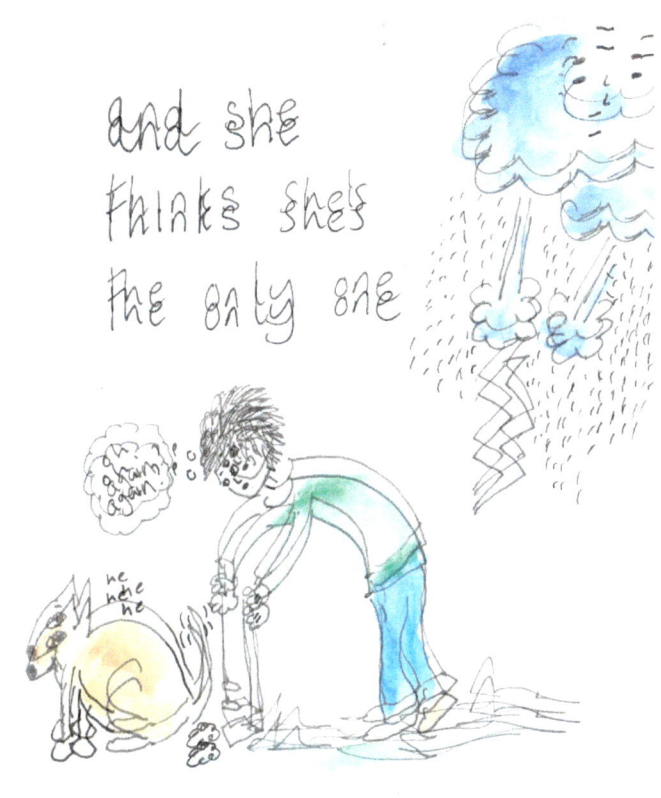

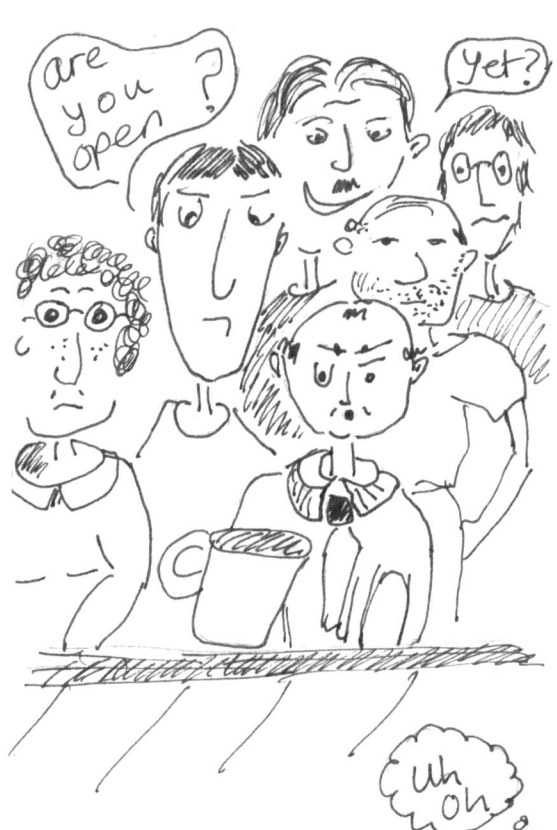

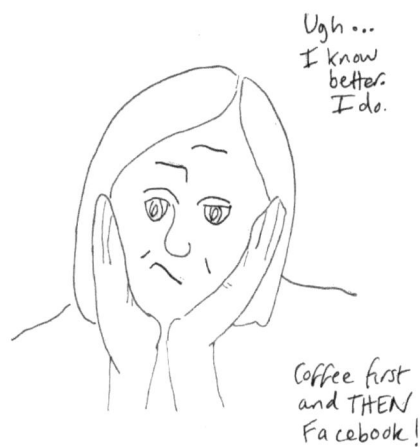

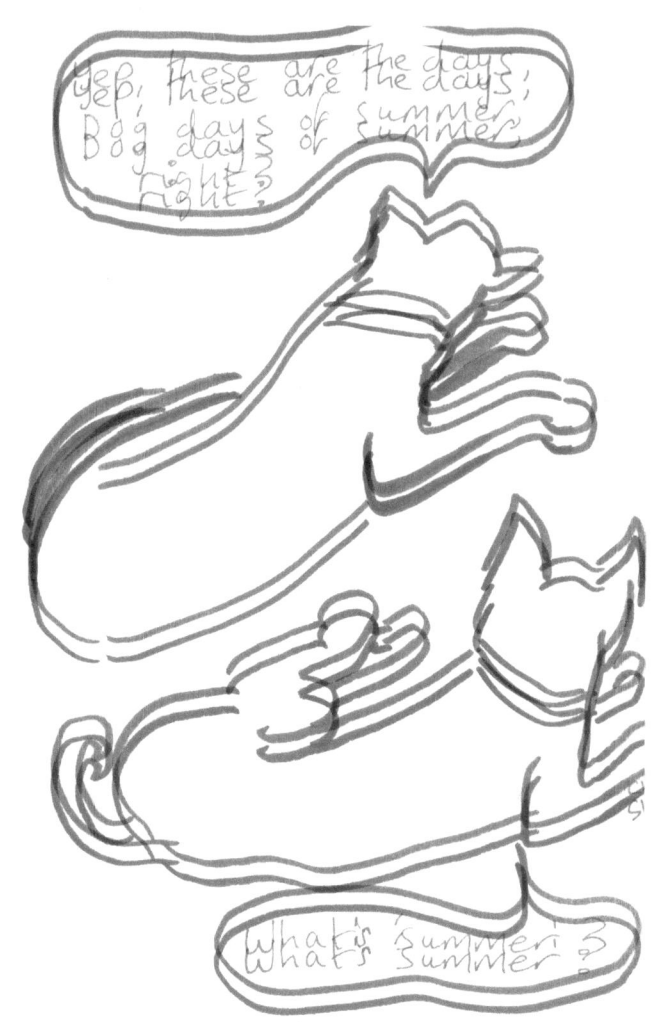

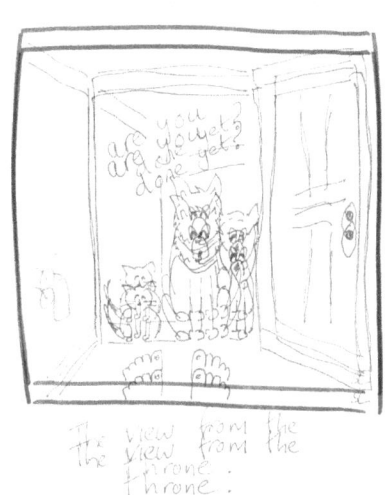

The view from the throne.

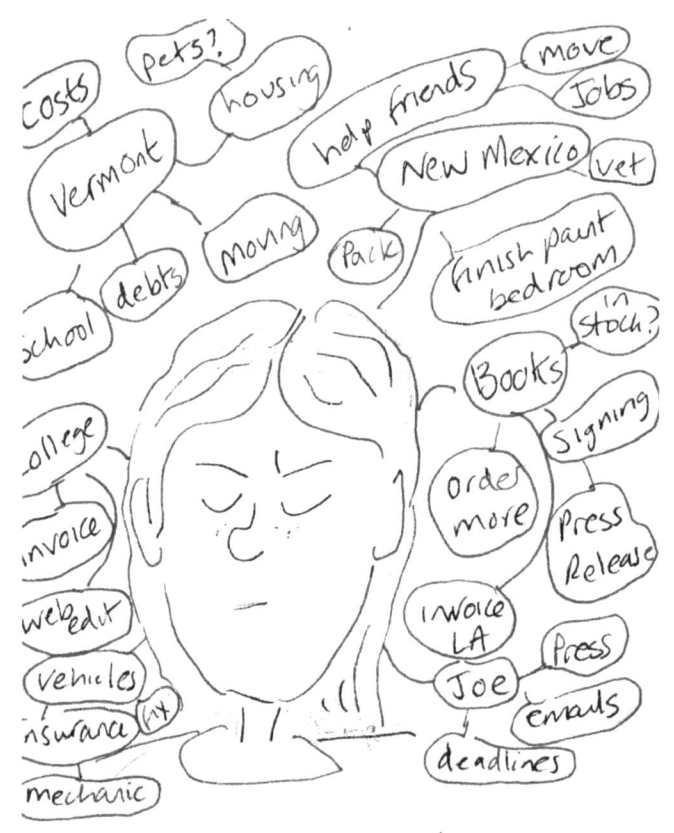

OH, THE JOYS OF MOVING

5/25/17

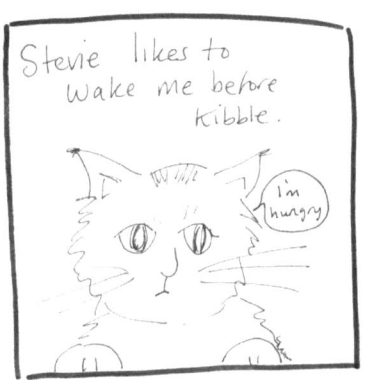

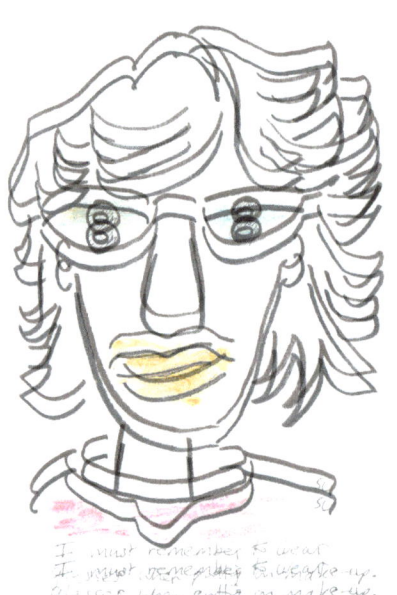

I must remember to wear
I must remember to wear my
glasses when putting on make-up.

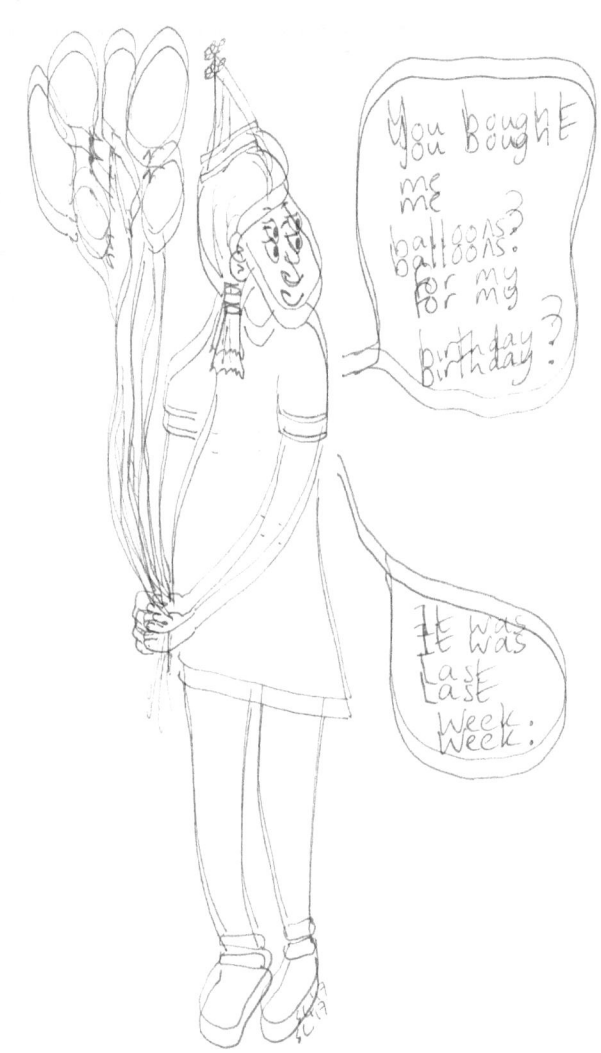

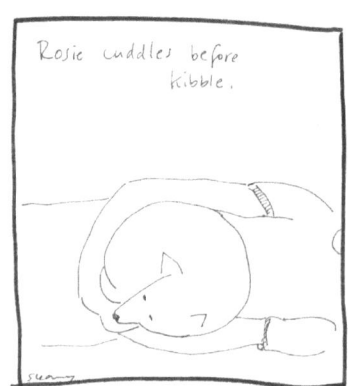

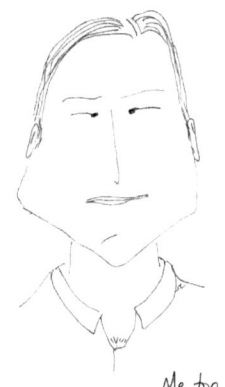

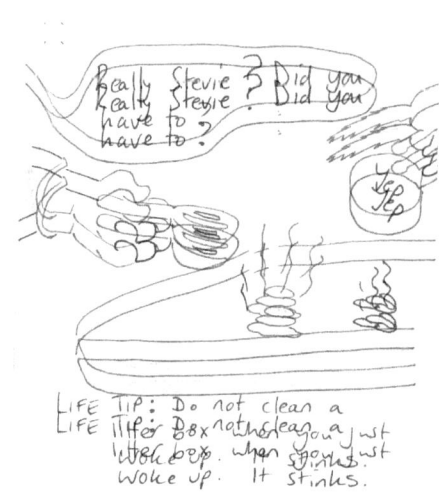

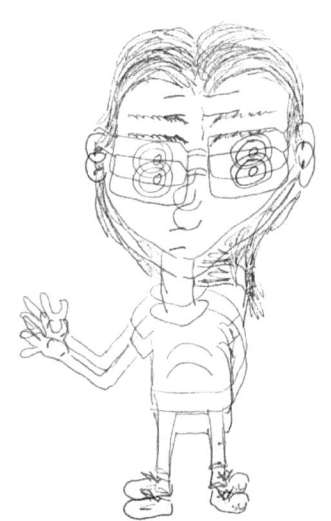

It's hard work being a writer;
Look how strong my hand is.

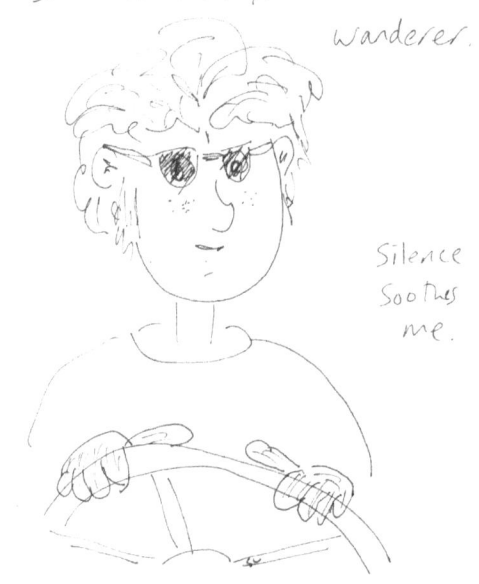

I shall always be a solo wanderer.

Silence soothes me.

Movement soothes me.

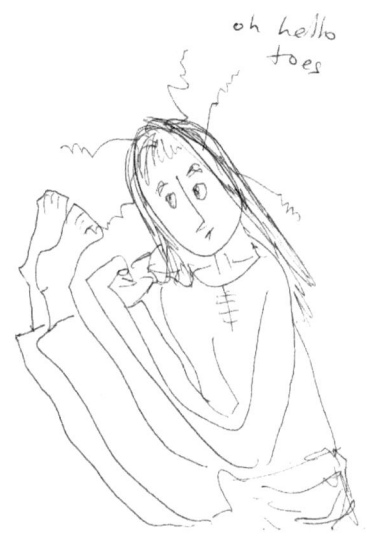

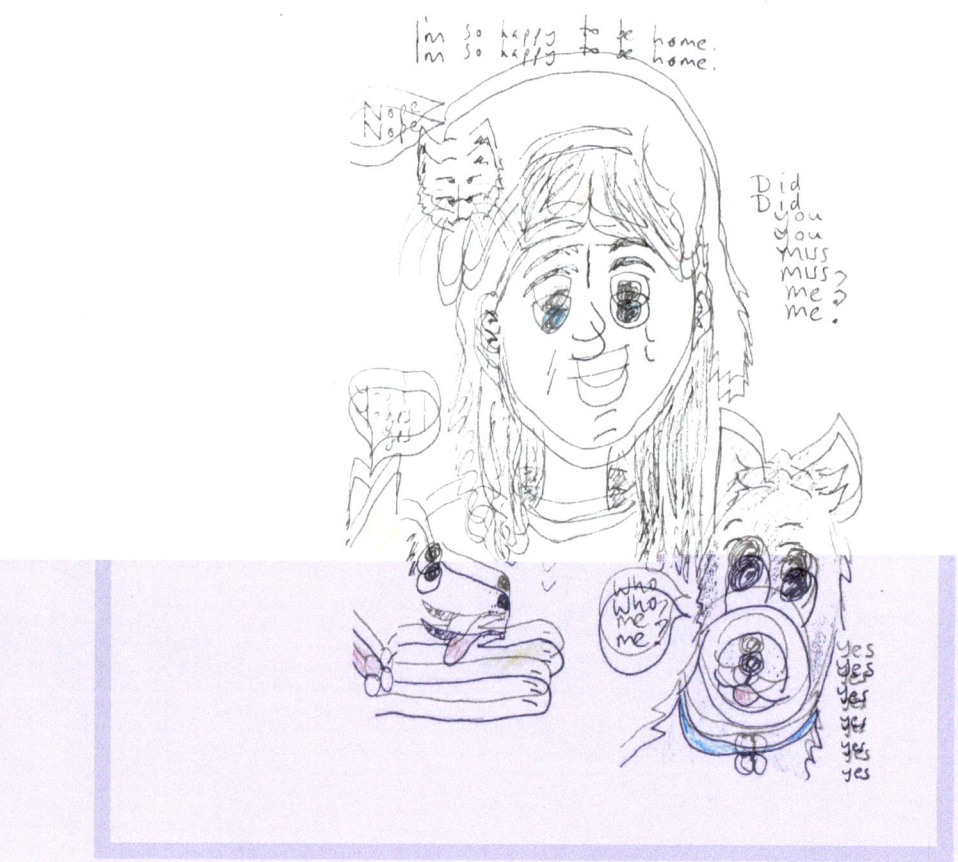

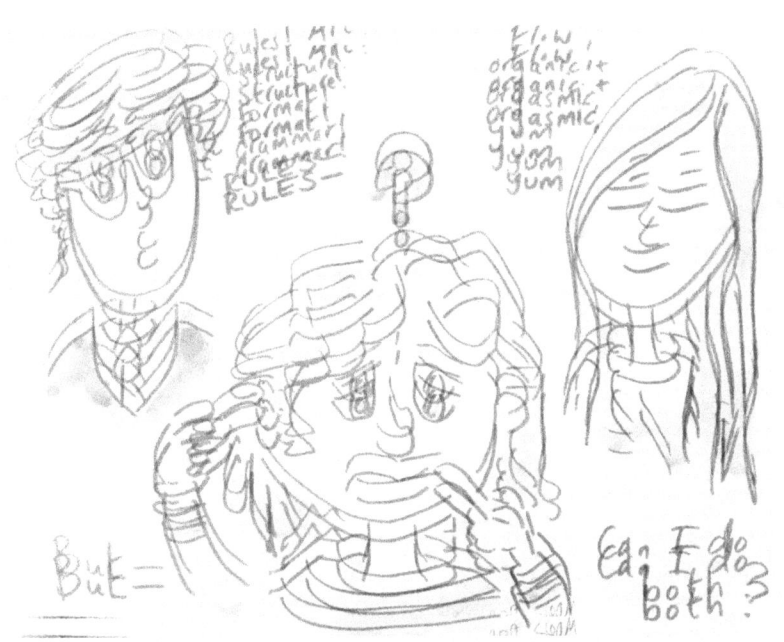

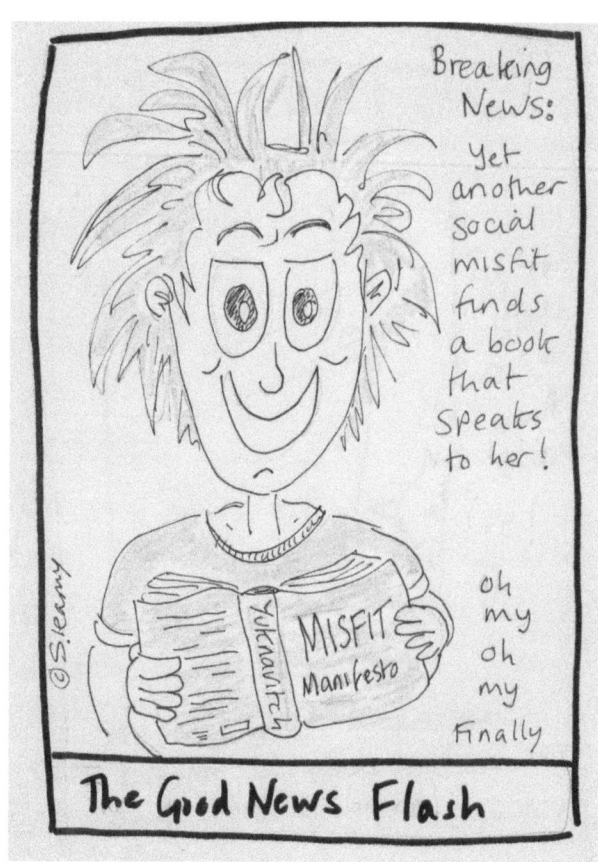

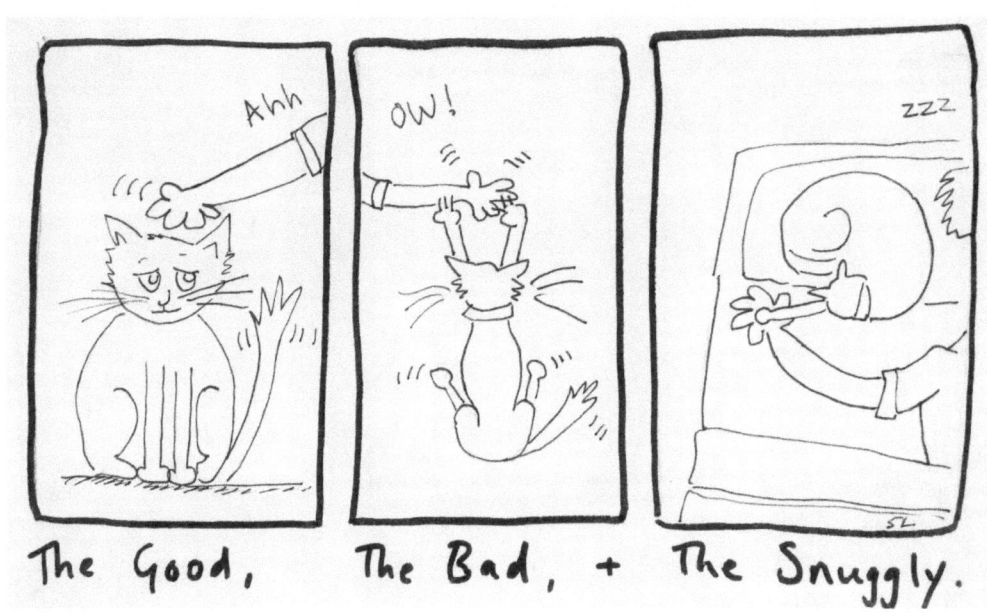

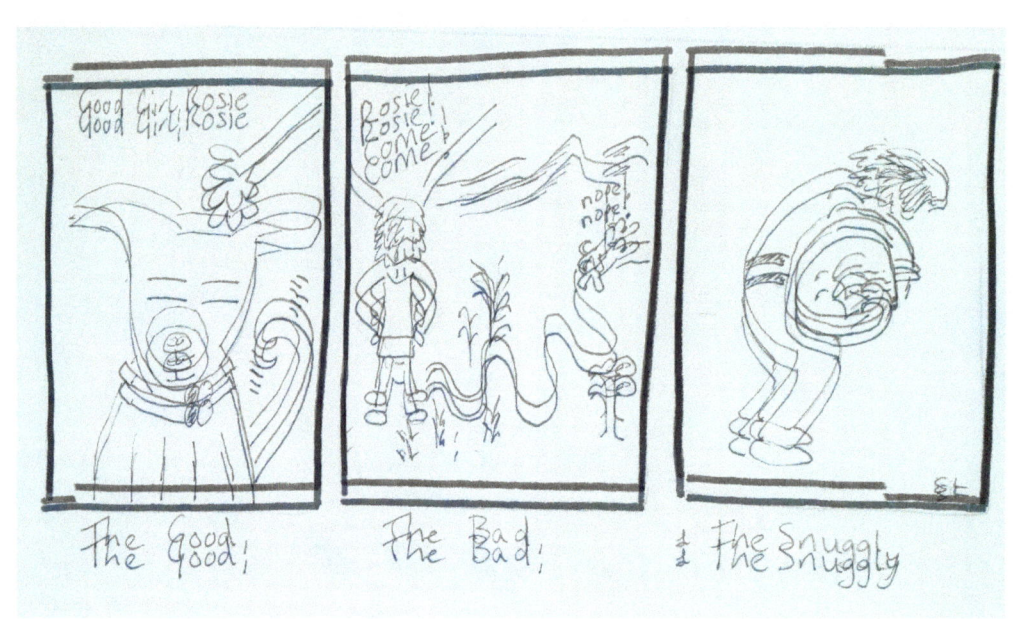

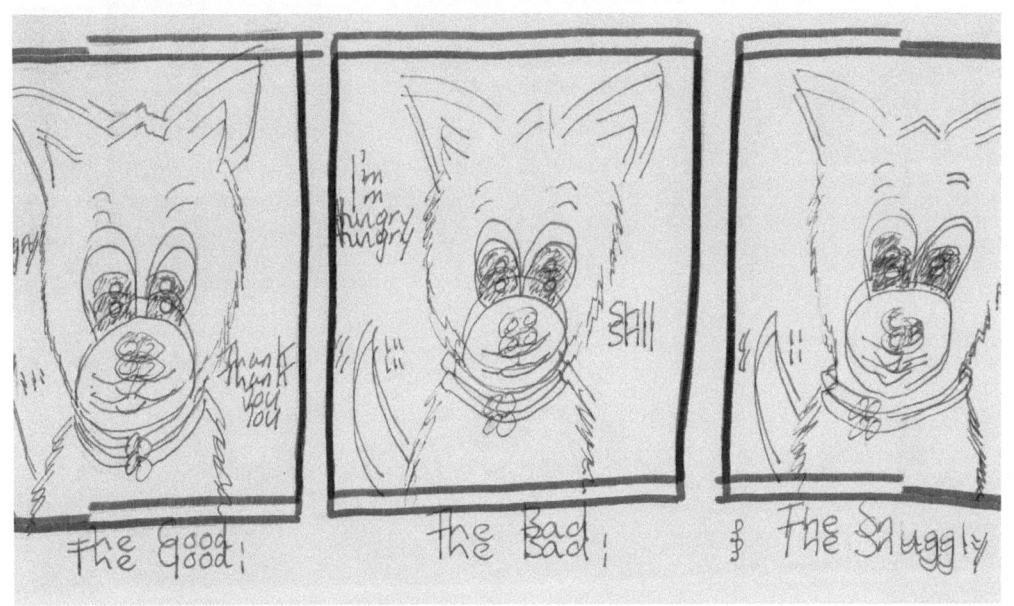

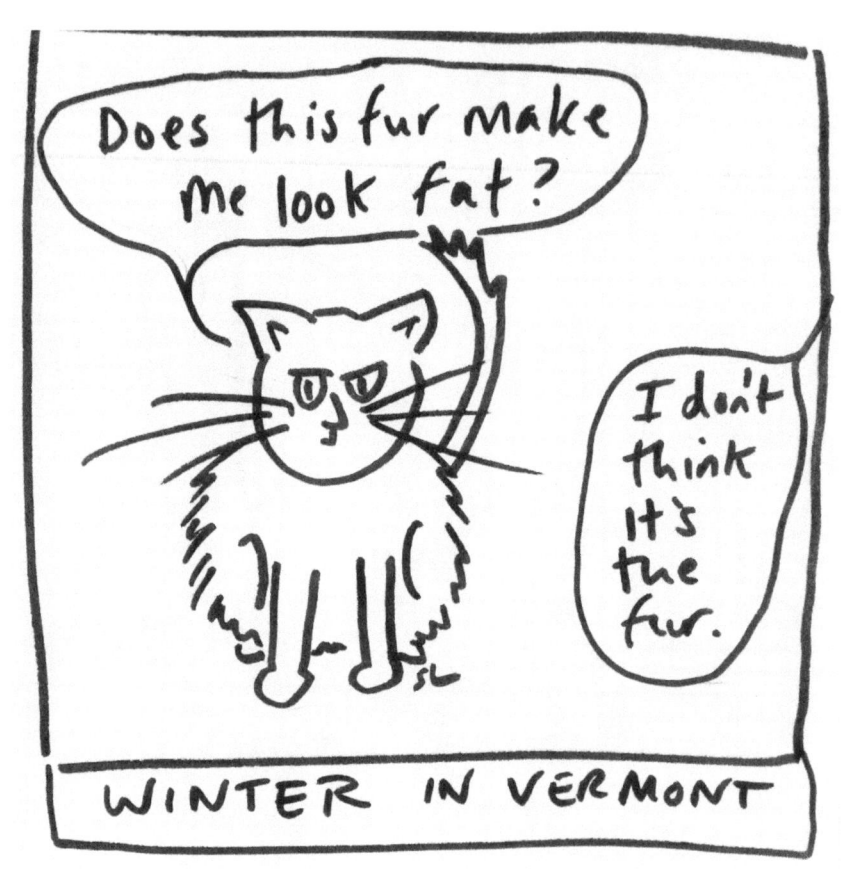

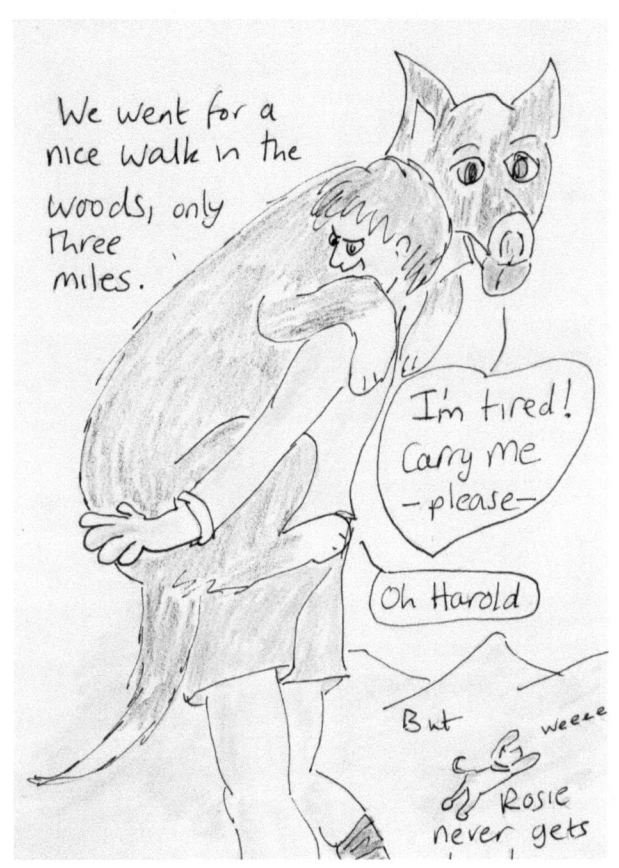

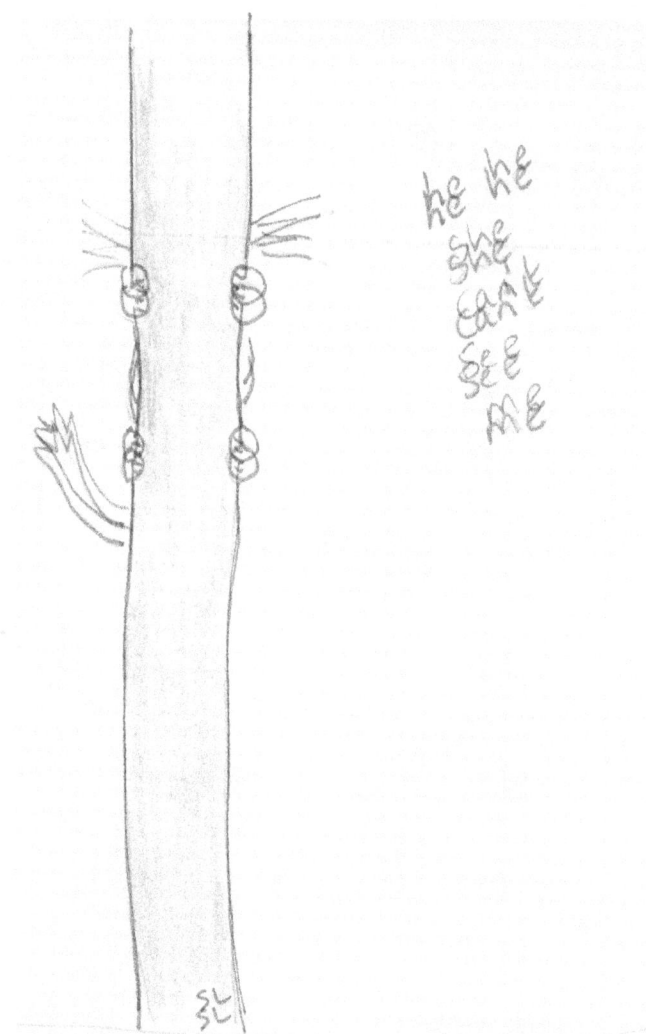

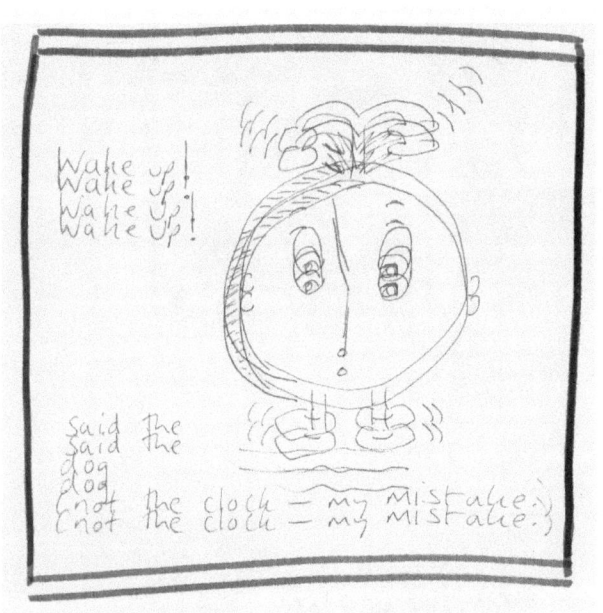

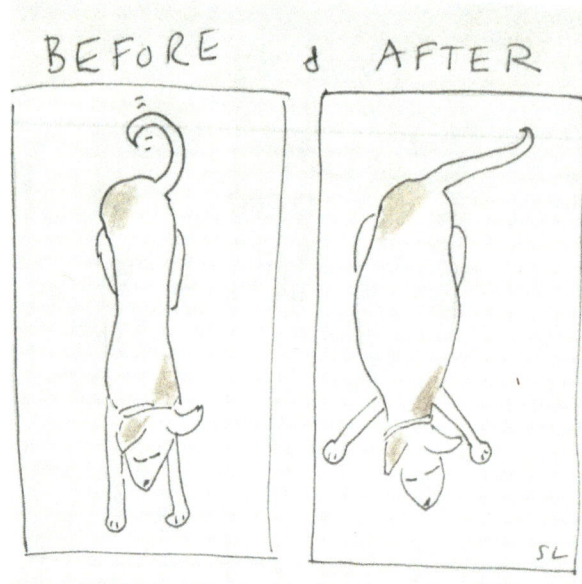

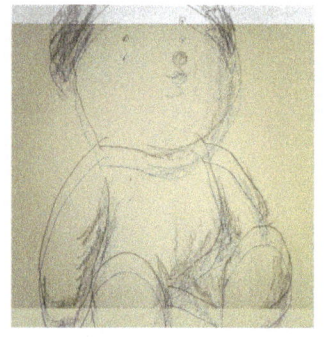